The Beauty of Black Women

ELIJAH JONES

authorHOUSE

AuthorHouse™
1663 Liberty Drive
Bloomington, IN 47403
www.authorhouse.com
Phone: 833-262-8899

Published by AuthorHouse 01/22/2021

ISBN: 978-1-6655-1499-6 (sc)
ISBN: 978-1-6655-1509-2 (e)

Library of Congress Control Number: 2021901282

Print information available on the last page.

This book is printed on acid-free paper.

Contents

Preface

In writing this book, The Beauty of Black Women, my goal was to uplift and encourage black women and girls because black women and girls need to feel like there are loved and protected. I have to admit that as a black man, I haven't always done that and I wanted to Change that so I wrote this book. I hope and believe this will change the lives of Black women and girls all over the world and give them a sense of hope and of self-worth because black women and girls you are worthy and you are treasured.

In writing each poem, I learned a lot about showing love and appreciation for the women and girls I care about. I also realized how black women have always been a source of inspiration and strength and that is why I personally dedicated each poem that I've written to all black women worldwide because I value black women and could not imagine a life without black women in it. Black women you are more than just stereotypes of being hood and ghetto because there is so much beauty in who you are as women from your hips to your lips and chocolate brown skin there is true perfection complexion.

I pray that, The Beauty of Black Women, does all that I can to honor you and give you as much praise as you could ever hope for and need. Another reason for why I wrote this book was because the overall perception of black women in America and the world for that matter has not always been a good one and The Beauty of Black Women aims to challenge the social norms of how people perceive and look at black women. Again, my goal for this book of poems is to change the narrative by painting black women in a more positive light and never looking down on them because the world and even black man tend to tear down black women rather than lift them up.

Incredible

Black Women You are truly
Incredible and if you were
Flowers I would eat you like
An edible and you are more than

Amazing truly more than a man
Could ever need and ever ask for
Because you are more than worthy
And truly unbreakable and all the

Love that I as a man have for incredible
Black Women like you are just unshakeable
And Black Women you are more than just beautiful
And are truly irreplaceable females to ever shine

In all lifetimes for all time and one day I hope and
Pray that God would allow me to call one of you
Beautiful black women out in this world my wife
Because my life would not and could not be the same

Without you incredible black woman like you around
Because black women you can't just be my anything when
I as a man need you to be my everything truly my light
Hope and strength for all time because I as a man want your

Love from incredible black women
Like you and I will forever need
Love from incredible, black women
Like you

Beautiful just Beautiful

Black women you are beautiful just
Beautiful to a man like me and black women
you truly a beautiful sight to see
And I can see is the heavens majesty

When I see you and when I think about
You and I have visions of your love
And I wrestle in the night when it comes to
My very thoughts of you kind of like Jacob in the

Night I can't leave without leave and live
Without your love and your everything
And all I want is for you to be all mine
Because you're very being is what I have long

Awaited like the corning of Jesus and as I
A man has always stated my love for you
Is furious and undebated and its only for you
And when I think about you l feel like I'm drowning

In the seas of your unending love and grace and
I feel like I'm drowning my emotions so deep
That I can't even sleep at time without thinking
Of you and all that you do and I'm going to be honest

And it has taken me many years
Of crying and at times denying
Myself of love and my own
Tears and it is only now that

Now see that in and around you
Heart is where I want to
Forever be because, black women
You are truly beautiful just

Beautiful to me so open your
Heart mind soul and being
For me so you can be my
Everything for all time

At The Table of Emotions

Look black woman all I want is a man
After your own heart and at the
Table of emotions is where I play
The role of the good guy since good

Guys finish last I might as well play
That kind of part because at the table of
Emotions is where I might get my start to
Truly be open and honest with a potential

Female in whom I can see myself calling
Bae because like I've said before my whole
Heart is only one heartbeat away and at the
Table of emotions maybe someday a female

Will see me for me and all my clay and maybe
At the table of emotions, I may never again be left afraid
Because opening up my heart has at times only left me played
And maybe at the table of emotions is where I can maybe deal

With all the shade hurt and pain so long as I don't
Break bend or fade away because black women I just
Want you to want me and for you to forever show love
To me because all I want is peace and to find rest and joy

In your loving arms because
In you black women I just
Want and long for embrace
And everlasting majesty

At the table of my emotions

My Heart Belongs To You Part 1

Black women whatever you need from
A man like me and my heart I as a man
Will not fail to do why because my heart belongs
To you because black women to me you are more

Than a man could ever want, an your love is
More than I as man could ever need, and it is your
Love alone that I as a man see as divine like the heavens
Dew and I as a man want each and every part of you and

You're very being to be all mine because my very heart
Belongs to you because you are beautiful to me and to
Me you truly are amazing and the incredible and the
Irreplaceable love of mine and you are the very hope that I as

A man cling to because you, black women have always
Had my heart because my heart, black women belongs to
You and it always has, and it always will belong to
You because I as a man will forever care for you and

And I as a man will forever declare my love for you
Whether I'm standing in the mist of desert sands or
Broken lands, black women, my life has and will always
Be in your hands because my heart belongs to you.

My Heart Belongs To You Part 2

Black women whatever you need from
Me as a black man and whatever you want
From me as a man I will not fail to do
Because I must say that as a man my

Very heart belongs to you because you
Make me feel like a man and you make
Me feel so complete with your beautiful
Wonders and everlasting love forever sweet

Because it's truly never ending because it
Is and will always be forever concrete and this
Is why I give you my everything as a man
Because again my heart belongs to you

Because you more that a man like me could
Ever need and you are more than a man like
Me could ever want and therefore I will forever
Be with you and for you because it is your love alone that is and was

Made so damn divine and as a man I just want and need to be
Inside of your great love and make it all mine for all time
Because again my heart belongs to you and even my very soul
Sings and dances at the very thought of beautiful, black women
    like you

Because my heart belongs to you
Because black women, I want and need
You to know that you're not just
My anything because you are my

Everything and ever part of who
I am as a black man and human being
I give it all to you because black women
You are more than I can ask or think
Of and you will always be

My Very Soul Means Nothing

Look my very soul means nothing
If I don't have someone like you and
My very soul means nothing if I as a man
Couldn't cry for you because my heart

Truly belongs to you because you've
Been my everything and without you
I am nothing because what could I as
A man even begin to do if, black women

Weren't my solid ground and if I didn't
Have you I would be lost in the ways of
Love and would never be found and again
My very soul means if my heart couldn't ache

For you or even break for you because all my
Heart does is yearn for you because like a fire
My heart burns for you and my very soul means
Nothing if you are not my Beatrice and I your Dante

Because hell shall not have you because I refuse to give
Hell, dominion over you because my soul is and will be
Nothing if I as a man ever lose you my soul truly will
Be nothing without someone like you

Emotionally Transparent

Black women I know that your
Going to love what you love
And see what you see but is there
Any room in your heart and in your

Life for a man like me because I need
To know if you have room for me and
All of my emotions and inner feelings
Like flowers that often bloom because

I want to share my world with you
And declare my love for you since
lm being so emotionally transparent
With you because I don't have time to

Play games and I don't have time
To be left played nor be a deceitful
Man, who only throws shade because verbal
Attacks and setbacks will only leave you afraid

Of me and I just want and need you to much
To leave you and your very heart betrayed and
Again, since I'm being so emotionally transparent
I as man will never allow you to just fade because

I'd rather be cut down by
Life's very blade since I'm being
So open and so honest about me
Being so emotionally transparent with you

The Incomparable And the Irreplaceable

Black women everything that you
Are and everything that you could
Ever be is truly incomparable and
Beyond that irreplaceable and you

Black women you are the single greatest treasure
And being that any man in this world could
Ever find because, black women you are the
Incomparable and the irreplaceable and the

Future love and loves of my life because you
Were born so heavenly and so bright truly and that
Has always been the light that has
And will always be the light of this

World of mine because you are the single greatest
Being to ever be seen within mv human view and
To other females I truly love them but black women
I need you to know that there is no female above you

Because you are and have always and will always be
The incomparable and irreplaceable black women
In whom I love and will forever adore because again, black
Women you are the incomparable and the irreplaceable

The Fully Guarded Heart

Look I as a man have been without real love
For so long and all ever wanted to do is
Feel real love so very strong but yet my mind
Set is in and remains in problematic turmoil

And emotional scorn and all I've ever wanted was
A black women that I could love and be loved on and
Be with a man like me because I want for a woman
Like her to adorn me so that I as a man could adorn

Her and for many years I've played the role of the good
Guy because that's always been my part along with
Being in and out of relationships with this fully guarded
Heart of mine that past females aka mistakes wouldn't let

Someone like me shine now who can love me and truly
Make all mine when personal and emotional and expressions
Of honest transparency can't seem to be seen as divine or
    maybe
It just wants my fully guarded heart and its many ways that had

Crossed the final line in the first place and here my heart
Is crying out, black women, don't go don't go don't go
Because my fully guarded heart needs someone like you
To forever love it so hold me close and please don't let me go

Emotional Reflections

To you black women and you black women alone
Is to whom I as a man give all my love heart
Mind body and soul and loving affections because
It's always been females like you that have always

Been in each and every chapter of my life along
With its many intersections and females like you
Have always been my personal selections because
To females like you there are no objections nor

Will there ever be and when I as a man felt so lost and
Alone it was black women like you who gave me the strength
And the love to fight on and find that place called home
And when I as a man was up against the cold and cruel world

It was females like you who became my course and direction and it
Will always be females like you in whom I give my loving
Heart to always in these emotional reflections of mine and since
I will forever love and need females like you there will be no real

Days of bae less famines or emotional distress nor any rejection
Because my heart is all yours because it always has, and it has always
Belonged to you even in the mist of the darkest of all my racial
Transgressions and emotional reflections

Every Time

Black women you have always been there for me every time
And black women you have helped me when I felt as though I could
    not climb
Over life's obstacles and situations with out any fear or hesitation
And that is why I want honor you with this poetic affirmation

And the difference that you as black women made in my life is more
    than evident
And to honor you and adore you and share my love for you will
    always be my intent
And black women to you I will always be loyal honest and above all
    dedicated
And every time I write I want you to know that you are truly
    appreciated

And while I live my love for you as black women is something, I
    wont ever hide
Because black women you give me all of you and all that your love
    and embrace could provide
And if you never heard a black man say this then to you black women,
    I want to say thank you
For all that you have done and all that you continue to do

For me and for all black men and I am glad that you even came
Into this life of mine and that god had allowed for you to never leave
    it the same
And again, I want to say black women you have been there for me
    every time
And black women you have helped me when I felt as though I could
    not climb

Every part Of you

Black women every part of you from your stretch marks to your
  thighs is what I love and adore

And black women every part of is everything that I have yearned
  after and so much more

And black women I can truly see the god within you and so I reach
  towards that light

And black women I need to be surrounded by your warmth and
  embrace so damn tight

And above other women black women I will now and always put
  you first

Because if do not this heart and soul of mine might breakdown and
  then just burst

And I could never allow for you to walk out of my life because I just
  love you to much

And no other woman could ever feel like you feel and I only treasure
  your touch

And when I stand amazed and mesmerized by you that is when I
  know I am in eternal bliss

And that is the kind of feeling that you only get once in a lifetime so
  I never could dismiss

It because it is far greater than what one could ever hope to understand
  and truly gain

And on life's roller-coaster of a ride black woman all I want to feel is
  your pleasure passion and

Pain and if for no other woman black women my heart is beyond open
  and waiting for you

And when I lose my way and feel so alone, I know that I your always
  there to help me through

Because black women your hands have and will always be upon
  someone like me
And that is what these beautiful brown eyes of mine are slowly
  beginning to really see

And for all sins against you black women I personally want move
  past and try to atone
And I want you to know that my heart as never been cold to you as
  if I was just stone
And black women I know that my love and dedication for you may
  not always seem evident
But know that I am going through so many changes it is with you in
  where my time will be spent

Hope

Hope is finding rest
And safety within a black
Women's loving arms
Because the greatest place
In which any black man could
Ever be is in a black woman's
Arms and I could forever lay
In a black woman's arms
Because in those arms I feel
So, protected and in those arms
I never feel neglected and because
Of that there is no other place where id
Want to be because if I am not
Around black women and queens
Then it is not even a possibility and
So, to you black women I will forever
Say yes because this life of mine is
What you alone continue to love on and
Bless and where ever black women are
In this world is where true love and
Hope is and lives

Beautiful Brown Eyes

Black women you
Have such beautiful brown eyes
That I just adore and of your body
And being I only want more
And from the core I am crying for you
And black women I can feel your heart
Crying out for me and I need for you
Come and save because I can't live
Without you that is why my heart
Is crying out for you because it longs for you
And black women
Life and all its treasures that lead to
Wealth mean nothing without you
To have hold and love on and from
The day that I looked into those
Beautiful brown eyes I realized that
My life just would not be the same
Without you here with me right by
My side until the end of time
And black women your love is
All I have as a black man who
Loves and cares for you now and
Always

No one's Above Your Love

Black women no one in all of creation is above the light of you love
that could never be ignored
As I as a man play and persist and press on for you love and for your
shine
And a day in this lifetime without your being and love is something
that I couldn't afford

Because you are everything my everything my forever treasure and
great reward
As I long for all that you ladies can provide and pour out of your
hearts with love so divine
Black women no one in all of creation is above the light of your love
that could never be ignored

And in my eyes, you black women will forever get love from a man
like me and forever be adored
Because each and every bit of my being wants to be attached to your
very vine
And a day in this lifetime without your being and love is something
that I couldn't afford

As I write my thoughts and memories of you on my heart where it
is forever stored
And if there ever when this was not so then I as a man have truly
crossed the line
Black women no one in all of creation is above the light of your love
that could never be ignored

Because I'm so wrapped in all of my thoughts and feelings of you as
    if it was a cord
That keeps me tangled up in this relationship that I want with yall
    because yall are so damn fine
And a day in this lifetime without your being and love is something
    that I couldn't afford

And just to reach the realities of your higher calling is what I as a
    man move forward
Because black women I just want you to be all your and for you to
    be all mine
Black women no one in all creation is above the light of your love
    that could never be ignored
And a day this lifetime without your being and love is something that
    I couldn't afford

The Depths of My Heart Revealed

Black women see this lonely and broken heart of mine is what you
    alone have healed
And the depths of this heart of mine know being revealed
And a greater man is who you alone helped me to be
And know and forevermore will you alone hold the key

Because I want to love you every night and everyday
And I want to need you in such a special way
Because when all I see is darkness in sight
You have always been that light

And ever since the day that I met you
My endless love for you has grew
And with every bit of my hurt and pain put aside
I want to be your lover and your guide

Because I want to be what you need in your life
And I refuse to bring chaos and endless strife
Because loves forever song will be the song that we will both sing
As I make you my queen and my everything

Can I Be Your Everything

Black woman can a man like me be your
Everything and can I be the one that
You could have to hold and to love for
All time and could you fall in love with someone

Like me for all time because I want to know
If I can be that kind of man who can give
You all that you want and could ever need
Because I have so much love for you and I just

Hope that someday maybe one day you will
Have love for me the kind of undeniable love
Meant for just us and can I put you first in all things
Because what good is any man if I don't have his queen

And have you ever searched for a heart like mine and have
You ever found a heart like mine if not then can I be that man
The man that desires to be a man that you can love because I've
Been longing for someone like you whose touch could bring an end

To all my darkest of days and night because I want to be wrapped
In your arms and in your heart because I've been needing and wanting
For something so black women can you be that something more
     because
Need this void of not feeling and being without love to finally end so

I Need A Woman

I need a black woman that loves god and is so damn fine
And I want her to be the light to be my source
And I want a black woman whose love will always and forever shine

And be someone that I as a man can go out with and just dine
With and for her to truly be the direction when I as a man need to
    stay on course
And I need a black woman that loves god and is so damn fine

And I just want to be all hers and she would be all mine
And I'm just going to keep saying this until my voice grows hoarse
And I need a black woman whose love will always and forever shine

And whose love for me that won't switch up and decline
Because I'm willing to give my everything to you because it is you
    that I will personally endorse
And I need a black woman that loves god and is so damn fine

Because I just can't be with a weak woman that has no self-worth or
    a spine
And my love is all for you but it for damn sure won't be something
    that I as a man force
And I need a black woman whose love will always and forever shine

Because I can see the beauty and worth of your god given design
And because you, black woman are in my life, I no longer have to
    carry any past remorse
And I need a black woman that loves god and is so damn fine
And I want a black woman whose love will always and forever shine

I Want To Be In Your Space

No matter what I have to do black woman, I just want to be in your
   space
Because I want to be the kind of man that could forever be in your
   main squeeze
Because I as a man long for your unending and unfading embrace

As I seek for your loving touch and beautiful and elegant face
And features galore because black woman to my heart you have all the
   keys
No matter what I have to do, black women, I just want to be in your
   space

All my sorrows and all of my pain you black women could forever
   erase
And when I'm around you I feel like I can finally be at ease
Because I as a man long for your unending and unfading embrace

Because I love your beautiful skin clay and all of its everlasting grace
And majesty because black women you are the only type of female
   that I as a man want to please
No matter what I have to do, black women, I just want to be in your
   space

Because my mind body and soul long to reach your secret place
Because all I've ever wanted as a man was to feel your heavenly
   breeze
Because I as a man long for your unending and unfading embrace

And all the love that I have for you black women is something that I
    could never replace
Because you mean everything to me and this is what the man of god
    in my guarantee's
No matter what I have to do, black women, I just want to be in your
    space
Because I as a man long for your unending and unfading embrace

When I Found My Everything

Its forever warm in this heart of mine
And the breeze that I'm feeling truly feels
As if it was only the season of spring and I
As a man know that I have so much love to

Give and so much love to bring and I never
Had to question who I can give my love to
Because when beautiful black women had came
Into this open and at times broken heart of mine

Is when I as a man had truly found my everything
Because what Joy could be greater and what love
Could be sweeter if black women weren't the honey
In the honey combs that is my special treat and what

Greater emotional and transparent realities could make
A man like me feel so complete and can take away all
Of my gloom but black women who keep my very heart
From going boom and they are my personal reason why

I as a man even sing because again when black women
Had came into my heart and into my life that is when
I as a man had truly found my everything and black women
I need you to know that without your love alone my love means
    nothing

Incomparable

I'm saying this as open and as
Honest as a man can be
Black women in my personal opinion
Are truly beautiful and all to incredible

And amazing women that could ever exist
Truly everlasting and irreplaceable and
incomparable to all other races of females
And black women you can do no wrong and

Black women you can play my heart like strings and
Streams of an R&B song which has and will forever
Be wonderful to me and black women since you are
So incomparable I will give all my love to you

I as a man I will never place any other female above
You because you are everlasting, and you are the
Incomparable female for all time to a man like me
And I love you my forever thing

The Emotional Barrier

Black women I'm giving you my whole
Heart with all my emotions displayed
Butt still my emotional barrier is up
Because I don't want to end up hurt

Alone and betrayed and it's like I want
To give you all of my love but I'm so afraid
Of the verbal backlash and shade because my
Heart has been through enough and prices have

Been paid and so this emotional barrier has always
Stayed and I tired of being the loving negro cast
Aside and brought below when all I ever wanted was to
Was love all I got as a negro was what feels like never

Ending woe and this why you see these crying tears
Of mine flow that often flow and this emotional
Barrier of mine has by the day continues to grow
Until a true loving heart forces, the barrier to bend

Break and then finally go away forever
It's hard to let go of past hurt and maybe
Black women you can be that somebody who
Can take it all and can you be that somebody, black women

For You I will Cry

Black women for you and your heart
I give you each and every bit
Of my being because it all belongs
To you and whatever you want and whatever

You need as a real man will not fall to do'
Because as a man after your heart for
Your heart and your alone is what I cry for
Because for you, black women I will cry

And for you I as a man will die for you
Because I love you too much and can't
Allow even one tear to fall from your
Face because I want to be and needed to

Be your man protector friend and guide
And as your man I will provide for you
And I will shelter you and your weary
Heart because you are truly my love and until

The end of time you will forever be my one
And only lady of my life and I'll give all of me
To you because again for you and you alone I
Have lowered my guard and I pray it is never me in

Whom you discard because
I love black women and I
Need you black women and for you
I as a man will forever cry

Can Your Heart Last

Black women can your heart truly last in the mist of what feels like
unending pain
And black women can I be the kind of man that can take away all of
that pain and fear
Because I can put an end to all of your heartache and rain

Because in my love and in my love alone you will find and gain
All that you've ever wanted or have ever needed so please do not
shed one more tear
Black woman can your heart truly last in the mist of what feels like
unending pain

And I want you to know that I would never treat you or your heart
as if it was just a stain
Because I love you and I'm all for you and I just want to make that
clear
Because I can put an end to all of your heartache and rain

So black women just put your faith in me and I promise that the hurt
will not remain
In your life because when you're in need just know that I will appear
Black women can your heart truly last in the mist of what feels like
unending pain

Because it is my love for you black women that I as a man could not
even begin contain
And it is you and emotions and your being that I as a man will forever
revere
Because I can put an end to all your heartache and rain

And never will you have to fight for reasons that you can't even begin
to explain

To a man like me and it is never and forever that for you and your
love I will always be here

Black women can your heart truly last in the mist of what feels like
unending pain

Because I can put an end to all of your heartache and rain

Can You Lock it Down

Black woman you know that you have the keys to my heart but can
    you hold it down
Or will you also take what I as a man offer to you and throw it all away
Or maybe you'll be so clouded in your own emotions and start to drown

And it seems like when I try to make you happy you still frown
Or maybe it's just too hard to see a real woman with the actions in
    which you display
Black woman you know that you have the keys to my heart but can
    you hold it down

And will it be as a man in whom you chose to love or will you play
    me like a clown
With no thoughts of worries nor any amount of delay
Or maybe you'll be so clouded in your own emotions and start to drown

And maybe you'll just never realize just how much I love you when
    It you that I gave my crown
To and have made everything but in the process of all that will you
    not want to stay
Black woman you know that you have the keys to my heart but can
    you lock it down

And you could be apart of me and my in circle of town
Or will you make and then break my very being and tear apart my
    soul and make it pay
Or maybe you'll be so clouded in your own emotions and start to
    drown

And at times I felt so crippled in love by your being and your
    everything all around
Me and I just hope that you won't be just another female that make
    me fade away and decay
Black woman you know that you have the keys to my heart but can
    you lock it down
Or maybe you'll be so clouded in your own emotions and start to
    drown

The Last Time

Black women I just want your love to be all around
Me because ever since I gave you the keys to my heart, I've been so
open
And all I can do is think of your loving touch and lovely sound

And I'm so caught up in my thoughts and feelings for you that it feels
as though I've drowned
And with these thoughts of lust and sin I just want to be all up in
that skin
Black women I just want your love to be all around

Me because the queen of this heart of mine that share with you have
been crowned
The jewel that I forever treasure and praise and why do I feel such
chagrin
And all I can do is think of your loving touch and lovely sound

Because you've got that good flesh that my horny self wants to badly
pound
And I feel like I've said this before but why does it feel like my head
is about to spin
Black women I just want your love to be all around

Me but with my heart being as guarded as it is, I've put my love on
the rebound
Because my heart along with my emotions and being can't keep going
through this again
And all I can do is think of your loving touch and lovely sound

And this the last time that I want you to surround
Me with anything that I as a man see as cheap love because I'm not
    washed up like a has been
Black women I just want your love to be all around
And all I can do is think of you loving touch and lovely sound

So Good To Be In Love Part 2

Black women you make it feel so
Good to be in love and oooh without
Your love I as a black man would feel
So, lost so please do not ever take away

Your love because black women you
Make it feel so good to be in love
And to me it's more than a sensational feeling
That you as black women have given me

And as a black man I feel so gratified that god has let
Your light love and all that you are as women shine upon me
And by now its no secret that I love and adore
You because black women your more than necessary

In my life ooh black women, you make it feel so good to be in
Love and ooh without your love I as a black man
Would be lost and ooh black women do not ever take away
Your love because I need it like I need you in my life everyday

And thank you Detrick Haddon and Tim and Bob for
Inspiring and influencing this poem created and dedicated
To uplifting and encouraging black women worldwide
And thank you as black women making it feel so good to be in love

In Jupiter's Love

And In Jupiter's love is where I as a man want to just fly
And I let no one put an end to this forever song
And it can forever have my heart and soul until the day that I as a
    man die

With love so open and ready from the door that it could touch Jupiter's
    love
With you black woman, girls and you black woman alone is where I
    as a man truly belong
And In Jupiter's love is where I as a man want to just fly

And it is to this kind of love that I could never say goodbye
To because it has such a good and lovely heart that's so damn strong
And it can forever have my heart and soul until the day that I as a
    man die

And everything about you black woman my Jupiter love I
Honor and shoe the upmost respect and esteem even when you are
    dead wrong
And In Jupiter's love is where I as a man want to just fly

Because as a man I must do everything to be sure to fortify
You and all of your walls no matter how long
And it can forever have my heart and soul until the day that I as a man die

No longer do I hurt know the tears are joyful when I as a man cry
As this heart of mine beats for you my Jupiter love like a banging bong
And Jupiter's love is where I as a man want to just fly
And it can forever have my heart and soul until the day that I as a
    man die

Cool and Close

Black woman we could just be friends or could we be more than just
    cool
or greater than that and be more close
Or could will play my loving heart and its kindness for weakness
    like a fool

Because I need a woman that won't treat me harshly or cruel
Or lead me down the pathways of heartbreak and endless woes
Black woman we could be just be friends or could we be more than
    just cool

Because I just don't want to end up hurt again because I want you
    black woman to fill this hole
In my heart because you are the queen of my life that I as a man
    have chose
Or will you play my loving heart and its kindness for weakness like
    a fool

And all I want as a man is to be a man after your heart because that
    has always been my goal
And life and it being is all in your hands to have and to hold like a
    beautiful rose
Black woman we could be just be friends or could we be more than
    just cool

Because you are the queen of my life and you are the one and only
    crown jewel
And this is how my life moves because well life moves on as it goes
Or will you play my loving heart and its kindness for weakness like
    a fool

And I can't allow my heart and my emotions guarded to drown in
  your pool
Because of the actions of so many other females that tried so hard to
  keep me on my toes
Black woman we could be just be friends or could we just be more
  than just cool
Or will you play my loving heart and its kindness for weakness like
  a fool

A Black Woman's Heart

And I will always and forever treasure a black woman's Heart
Because in my life is where I need you to stay
And I pray that your sweet sweet love would never part

Because you black woman in my eyes are god's greatest work of art
Because you were chosen and worthy to be gods greatest clay
And I will always and forever treasure a black woman's Heart

Because you have always had my love ever since creations very start
And you are the very brightness to my very day
And pray to god that your sweet sweet love would never ever part

And I pray your beautiful brown eyes and chocolate skin and being
   never depart
Because you are a beautiful woman in every single way
And I will always and forever treasure a black woman's Heart

Because there's nothing in this world that could ever tear apart the
   feelings and love for you apart
Because you are my queen that I as a man will always put on display
And I pray to god that your sweet sweet love would never ever part

And you're very being is always high on my forever chart
Because my love for you black woman couldn't ever be in disarray
And I will always and forever treasure a black woman's Heart
And I pray to god that your sweet sweet love would never ever part

Upon Her Throne

And all I can see is a beautiful black woman upon her throne
And no one in all of creation can out match her very beauty and grace
Because she is an independent and strong woman all on her own

And she doesn't even need a man like myself because she's so fine
and so grown
And even I as a man don't always feel so worthy to even be in her
presence and enter her space
And all I can see is a beautiful black woman upon her throne

And I as a black man love everything about her and everything that
lies on her very bone
Because I've been longing for a black woman's loving and warming
touch and embrace
Because she is an independent and strong woman all on her own

And I love how she can take and dish out anything and everything
that is thrown
Her way because she as a woman has pride in every that she might
face
And all I can see is a beautiful black woman upon her throne

Even when the realities of life and death winds have blown
Against her she knows that she is nothing that life and death could
ever erase
Because she is an independent and strong woman all on her own

Because being a strong black woman is all that she has ever known
And even if I as a man ever step out of line, she will put me in my
place
And all I can see is a beautiful black woman upon her throne
Because she is an independent and strong woman all on her own

Heaven in your Eyes

Black woman in your beautiful brown eyes I can truly see the heavens
in your eyes
And it is the elegance and the radiance that I see within you that
always shines
And the love that I have for you is love everlasting and it never dies

And everyday of my life I long for you and to forever be in your
cloud nine skies
Because your beauty and your worth never declines
Black woman in your beautiful brown eyes I can truly see the heavens
in your eyes

Because your clay and your being that god allowed to be apart of my
life is like a grand prize
And that is what I as a man will forever treasure you because I want
you to be all mines
And the love that I have for you is love everlasting and it never dies

Because I am not the kind of man that would ever put you on the
sidelines
And black woman a true proverbs 31 woman is what your beings
alone always defines
Black woman in your beautiful brown eyes I can truly see the heavens
in your eyes

And as a man after your heart I love you and treasure your very rise
And I think about the time that I as a man spend with you as the
time flies
And the love that I have for you is love everlasting and it never dies

Because it's your actions that leave me amazed and so mesmerized in these cloud nine highs

That only you black woman could take me to because I want to crafted in your forever love vines

Black woman in your beautiful brown eyes I can truly see the heavens in your eyes

And the love that I have for you is love everlasting and it never dies

My Heart in Human Form

To the black woman who is
My forever lady you are
The only one for me and you
Are the only one in who I

As a man I give my very heart
And being to because black woman
You are and will always be my heart
In human form because from the

Beginning of time my very heart
And all my love that I as a man could
Ever have has been for you and you
Alone because my heart has always

Belonged to you no mattered the tests
And trails what felt like life's unending
Storm and storms and again you will
Always be my heart in human form and

And I as a man will forever have for you
And I as a man will always keep you in my
Heart and always give you my heart because
You, as black woman are and mean everything to a man

Like me truly my heart in human
Form and everything that I could
Ever need and want you, black
Women are to me because you mean

More to me and my very loving
Heart than this whole world and
For you black women will truly
Cry for you, black women

I will die because again
You black women will always be
My Heart in form and I will always
Love you because from you I as a man

Could never part

I Imagine Us

To that special black woman I imagine us being in loves
Forever chapter and I imagine us being in
That special setting fairy tale with a true
Happily, ever after and I imagine us with

Our very hearts being as one because all of
My life I've been trying to find someone like
You because as a man I've been in need of
Someone like you to hold and to love wild

Because I truly need you black woman and I
Truly need you black woman that can
Erase this broken and damaged heart of mine
And mend all the pain and rain in my life because

Until I met you for many years I as a man was
Drowning in my own tears and until I met you
I was drowning in my own fears until you carne
Into this world and life of mine forever blinding me

With the realities of true love leaving me with
No sight and I image us each other's arms and
Holding hands and being on the shores of jet black
Sands because in you I've found my everything and that

Has and will always be you black
Woman because I imagine us being
With each other forevermore
Because there's no other female that

I could ever love like I love you
And there's no other female that I could
Need tike I need you because, black
Woman with no other female can I go

Through life's open door with
But you and you alone because that's
What I imagine us being and doing
As these thoughts echo in my head

I'm the Man

Look Black women I've been wanting and
Needing you all of my life even through
All of my right as a man and even through
My wrong and even through all of my love

And lust because I love you and I hate to see
The tears fall from your face because black
Woman you are what no real man should ever
Disgrace and if you need true love let me be

Your black teddy bear and your lover and
Your very embrace because I can be the man that you
Need and I can be your shine and I can be your
Very heart and if real love is what you are trying

To find then you can find it in a man like me
And from now until the end of time I'll be here
Because I truly love you and give you all the
Praise that I as a man could ever give to you

Because you black woman are more than enough
Woman for all days so just reach on out and
All the man that I am will be here because I'm
The man that you've been in need of but the question is

Will you be ready and willing
To receive my love look here's
My life's very journey so take a look
I as a man I'm more than

Qualified and here I am
Today telling you I'm am
That man and I'm all that you
Would you're all that I could

Ever want

I'm The Man Pt.2

Black women my loving heart is more than ready
To be loved on by you and you
Alone because I care for you and
Love you and there's not a man

Like me on this earth that you could
Ever find like me because there's only one
Me so what don't you black women, choose
A man like me when I can be all the man

That you need and I can be your lost shine
And I can make your genuine and unfailing
Love all mine and I can be your heart if true love
Is what your trying to find so just come over to me

And fly over my way so that my heart can reach you
Heartache and wipe each and every tear that you've ever
Had all away because whenever you are my love is where
I must be yes, I must be the for you and all of your love for

All time so please black women please just open your
Heart and your mind for a man like me and say from
The very depths of your loving being that I'm the
Man, that you want and need and all you will ever want

Under Pressure

Black woman know that I love each
And every part of you because your
Love rains down like the heavens dew
And even the angels are in awe of you

And I'm so under pressure to tell you
Just how much l love want and need you
All around me and in my life and in this
Heart of mine and what I as a man truly

Think of you because there truly are no
Words that I can really say because at
This point in my life my heart is only
One heartbeat away from you and

Every day and night I think about you black
Woman and each and each and every
Night I dream about you, black woman
And how I want you right by my side and

I'm Forever in my feelings and drowning
In my own emotions of wanting and needing
Your everything because that's how it's always
Been when I talk and think about you black woman

Breaking My Fortified Wall

Black women will you alone be
Answering the call of breaking
My fortified wall and will you have
Time to hear me when I as a man have

To cry out or will you just walk out of
My life and pass me by because I need to
Know whether or not you will be on my side
And I need to whether or not I'll have to shield

Myself in my own pride and I need to know
Whether you can wipe away each and every
Tear in which I as a man have cried because I'm
Forever on guard when it comes to my heart and

I will never again let a female play my heart because
I just want to be held and to be loved and to never
Again, feel like in this world alone and I never again
Want to be denied so again black women will you answer

The call of breaking my fortified wall or will you
Be like other females who only want to see a man
Like me just fade away slowly and fall so, black women
What will it be everyone else around you or a man like me

Let Me Be The Clay Pt 2

Here I am back again giving praise
Giving praise honor glory to one of
My favorite types of females and that
Is black women and with that being said

I'll begin this poem by saying this black
Women here I am again pouring out
All of my inner most feelings and emotions
To say this, I have the same question as before

But this time black women, I need an answer
Asked you can you let me be your black teddy bear
and your lover and your true embrace and will you let me be
The clay that makes its very way to your heart because

I as a man figured that you would let me in because I'm
Not like other men who came at you with sex and
Smooth conversation and sin because know that if I had
Done the same it would be your heart black women that I as

A man could never win and if I had as a black man had you
I could only win and never lose because black women you're all
That I want and all that I could ever choose so please just
Let me be the clay that can be all that you could want and need

The Only One for Me

Black women my love for you
And you're very being is incomparable
To any other man that you've ever loved
Or have ever met and my very heart of all

The man that I am and will forever be has always
Belonged to you since time even had a say and
Had begun and all I ever did as a man was play my
Part and looked at my reflection to make an honest

And faithful man out of myself so that one day I could
Give you all of my love with each and every beat of
My loving heart because beautiful and lovely black
Women you know that my heart belongs to you and you alone

Because this love that I have for you is a forever
Thing to the girls that I as a man give my everything
To and you are who I give the key to so you can go
Through the door and find my lovers everlasting majesty

Because black women truly are the one for a man like
Me because you make me feel loved and treasured
In worth and honor that no being in this world could'
Ever have because black women you are the only one for me

Walk on Water

Black women you are truly wonderful to
Me and you are beautiful to me and you're not
Just anything like other females that I as a man
Would only cast aside because black women you are

My everything truly the only women that I could forever
Adore because you and your very clay and being mean
Everything to me and in my eyes, you seem to forever walk
On water but even in the mist of my darkest of days on this earth

You could still never be Jesus and to me your so much more than
Human to me and you're the only type of females for a man like me
And even the blind can see that I will always and forever have love for
You for all eternity because you're all that I've longed for my whole
    life

And your all I've needed my whole life because you've been all that
    I've
Ever needed as a man and as a man knew I needed you when I
    looked at
You like you would look at heavenly angels ascending and descending
    from
The heavens above who shower me down with the power and might
    of gods

Love even though you black women walk on water you still could
    never
Be Jesus and in your heart mind and soul and being is where I as a
    man will
Forever drown because I love you black women and I as a man will
Forever hold you down because you black women walk on water

Giving You The Best That I Got

Now black women I know that I am no
Anita baker but I as a black man ill forever
Be giving you the best that I got because if I do not
Then another man and I can't have another man come and

Take my place when your heart is where I've always
Wanted to be because black women only women like
You could love hold and provide for me in such a special
Way and that is more than any words could ever say

And that is why I will always be giving you the best that
I got and no matter what I say or do black women your
Love has always come to my rescue and now that all
This love that I have for you as black women was meant

To be and black women I'll never stop giving you
The best that I got because I know that you will never
Stop giving me that you got because black women you
Truly have so much love for me and I know that it will never stop

The Void In My Heart

Oh, black women
Only you can fill the void in
This lonely heart of
Mine because black women its
Always been about you and
Only you love can fix
A man like me and
Only your love can mend
All of brokenness and
All this pain that I
Continue to feel and maybe
That is why I can see the god
In you because when I cried
Out black women you had
Answered the call and black women
You alone were there every time
I did fall and that is why
Only you as black women can
Fill the void within
My heart

My Something More

Black women you need to know that you have and will always be my
   something more
And I truly mean that from depths of my heart and its emotional core
And every since you step foot in my life you had me open from the
   door
And it feels like my heart is beating so fast and I know that it your
   making
It feels like it can soar

And for your love black women like a lion I will forever roar
And black women you will always be the women in whom I adore
And on everything in me as black man is what I swore
And black women your more than what any man could ever for

And black women being in your loving arms of embrace feels so
   damn right
And it is a feeling that my heart cannot explain nor ever choose to
   fight
And black women you are the greatest and most valuable treasure
   in sight
And if I could I would shower down every black woman with all my
   love and might

And when I think speak and write you as black women It will always
   be with vigor
Because I do not just want to uplift and encourage it is your very
   beings, I want to restore
You as black women because you have and will always be my
   something more
And I truly mean that from depths of my heart and its emotional core

Everything That I'll Ever Need And More

Black women if no other man has ever told you this
I want for you know that you are and you will
Always be everything that I'll ever need and more
And black women you are the mind objector

The heart protector and the soul defender of anything
That I as a black man could ever fear and you are
The baby conceiver and the only real women that could
Ever make me a believer the joy bringer and lover giver

Black women you are and I want to always honor you
And adore you because black women you are everything
That I'll ever need and more and for you alone I will be the
Man, that you've always need for me to be because without you there
    is no

Me and without you there is no what can be and even blind
Eyes can see that I have so much love for you and that you as
Black women have so much love for me and that is why I have
Share this with you today because black women I love you and

I need for you to continue to love and hold me down
And black women you are everything I want and black women
You are so much more than what I thought could ever be
And black women you are the pain remover and bad times undoer

The Running Oil

And black women do you remember when a sinner like me came to
you in the mist of all my turmoil
Wanting you and needing you to take away all of my hurt and pain
Because my tears and scars have also ran deep like the running of
the oil

And how you Oh black women you always where there when I need
someone's love wrap me up like foil
So that I would no longer feel as though I've lived in vain
And black women do you remember when a sinner like me came to
you in the mist of all my turmoil

So that my body mind and soul would forever be planted in your
good soil
And because of that I'm much stronger then that after the rain
Because my tears and scars have also ran deep like the running of
the oil

And Thank you Oh black women melanin in heaven for shielding me
from all of life's recoil
And now I know that there is truly more of you for me to love and
adore in my own lane
And black women do you remember when a sinner like me came to
you in the mist of all my turmoil

And my sins where at the highest temperature when your anger
against me would boil
Because it was I alone who had tired so hard to jump off of your
very train
Because my tears and scars have also ran deep like the running of
the oil

And at one time in my life my personal sins and ungodliness is how
    I used to toil

Because before I met you, I was out here in this world acting
    belligerent and insane

And black women do you remember when a sinner like me came to
    you in the mist of all my turmoil

Because my tears and scars have also ran deep like the running of
    the oil

The Incredible True Story

Black women I knew a man who
Would give you his everything even
If it left him with nothing and I knew
A man who chase after your heart and

Allow nothing in all creation to come
Before you or above because nothing in
All creation will tear all that apart because
Black women I need you to let me love you

Because I have so much love for you and
You alone because black women you are the
Only queen worthy and found honorable
Enough to be a queen upon my throne because

I'm tired of all the tears and all the lies and
All the words said whether it was in the past
Old things at a certain point in my life just
Grows dead and I hate to see you black women

Hurt and misled because all I've wanted to be
Was man after your heart because a man after
Your heart should cry for you and a man after your
Heart should die for you instead because I will be that

Kind of man if it means that I can
Has your heart and love alone
Because I will more than bare all of
Your pain and I as a man will put an

End to of your rain because the
Man that cries for your heart
Only wants to see you shine
In everlasting, glory divine

And that to me as a man
Is the incredible true story
Because black women I don't think
You understand just how much

Love that I as a man truly have
For you

The Incredible Amazing and the Irreplaceable

Black women you are the
Most incredible amazing and
Irreplaceable women that ever could live
And ever will live and you forever stay on my

Mind and your all I as a man have been trying to
Find and my heart and my very life as a black man
And as your future lover is in your hands because you
Love is strong and concrete and nothing in this world could

Be as sweet as your love and it is your love that.
Makes my heart beat because black women you are
Not just my anything because you're like no other because
My whole heart mind being and soul is more than ready

To make you my everything because black women you where
Born and made to be my everything which other females could
Never be nor even play the role because black women you will forever
Play in that position because black women you are my open door

And when I as a man had because lost ins this cold world it was in
You black women that I was found and then was made new and that
Was also the day that you black women became my forevermore
    because?
You are and will always be the incredible amazing and irreplaceable

Women in my life who will
Forever shine because my
Heart is forever yours and
Your heart I hope and pray

Is forever mines and mines
Alone you incredible amazing
And forever irreplaceable
Black women

To Be In A Room Full Of Black Women

Look to be in a room full of black women
Is the greatest feeling on earth standing and being?
Around beautiful chocolate melanin queens is what I treasure
And to reach a black woman's chocolate high
Is like crack to me so I must be the fiend and I am
Trying to make the point clear so you know
What I mean and being around black women
Makes my life feel so serene and I just want
Love on black women beyond what any words
Can say because my actions will always speak
For what my words cannot convey and to be in a
Room full of black women is where I know true
Love runs deep and the key to my heart is
What black women will forever keep
Because black women you know how to make
My heart skip a beat and my thoughts of who
You are as women is like your chocolate brown skin
So lovely and forever
sweet

When Heaven Met Earth

When black women entered this
World that is when heaven met earth
And black women you and you alone have
Always had true melanin beauty and infinite worth

And no other woman could ever do the
Things that you do amazing you and
Black women you are more than what
Words and actions could ever describe over

Ever even define and even the very angels is who
You as black women outshine and I know that
My last verse might have crossed the line
But black women to me you are just that beautiful and fine and

Black women I will forever respect and admire
You and your richly melted chocolate skin
And natural curves and endless wonders and more
Because black women my heart has always belonged to you

And black women you are and will always be the
Greatest beings that god could have ever called forth
To birth and black women the very reason why heaven even
Met earth and for that I always love honor and adore you black
    women

So Good To Be In Love

Black women you make it feel so
Good to be in love and oooh without
Your love I as a black man would feel
So, lost so please do not ever take away

Your love because black women you
Make it feel it so good to be in love
And to me its more than a sensational feeling
That you as black women have given me

And as a black man I feel so gratified that
Your light love and your all has shined upon me
And by now its no secret that I love and adore
You because black women your more than necessary

In my life ooh black women, it feels so good to be in
Your love and ooh without your love I as a black man
Would be lost and ooh black women do not ever take away
Your love because I need it like I need you in my life

And thank you Detrick Haddon and Tim and Bob for
Inspiring and influencing this poem created and dedicated
To uplifting and encouraging flack women worldwide
And that's why it feels so good to be in love

A Man after Her Heart

With her and her love alone I pray
That as a man I will never part because
Lord I just want to be a man after her heart
And I pray that you reveal my open and ready

Heart to love someone like her forever more
Because she's not like any other female because
She is my everything and not just my anything truly
The only woman in my life and the only one for me because

I dream about her and I think about her and all I want
To do as a man is love on her and kiss her because
I need all of her and to give her all my everything as a
Man, because again with her all her emotions feelings and

Heart I as a man could never part from them because
I desire to be a man after her heart because my for her is
Kind and my love for her is true and it was made for beautiful
Black woman and for you for your eyes only know

Forevermore because as a loving black man I cry for you and all
I want to be is a after your heart because your
All could ever want to love and to hold you and need and
I need you my heart needs you and my very being
to hold and love always

Say Yes

Black woman I as a man have so many feelings that
I need to express but at the same time what I
Need for you to do is open up your heart and say
Yes, to a man like me because the last thing that I

Would want you to do is second guess the very idea
Of us being together and all and I just want to know
Will you love me and do you have love for me and if
So, will you just open up your heart to me and just say yes

Because there's not another man in all of creation that you
Could ever find like me so please don't keep me and my heart
And emotions waiting or have them left behind because I as a man
Don't want any more pain or added stress about whether or not you
     will

Say yes to me giving you all that I am as a man because I want to give
You what you've been wanting and waiting for but I need for you to
Just say yes because I just want to be in your everlasting love so deep
And divine and finally have all of you but only if you could just say
     yes to a man like me

From My Heart To Yours

From the bottom of my heart and soul as a man
These love poems of truly beautiful verse are like
Are songs that I could forever sing to you because
I love and will forever think about you because black women

My love for you shines even brighter than the sun
And when I had met you that was when my life had
Truly felt as though it had just begun and like Brian
McKnight if ever I believe that my work as a man is

Ever done then I to will start back at one because everything
In me as a man longs for and cries for you and only you and from
My heart to your heart you know that what I say is true because
    everything
That you are and everything that you could ever be has truly made
    my dreams

Come true and with every beat of this heart of mine and every
Word that I could ever say I as a man will always and forever
Be one heartbeat away because without you being in my life
I would feel and be left so incomplete and with you alone I want to

Get lost in love's forever shores because that is where I want
To be and from my heart and soul you can forever be mines
And I can be all yours now and forever because you will always
Be in this open and loving heart of mine

The Emotional Rainbow Butterfly

Look for you and you alone
Have I shed many tears and
For you and you alone I've tried
So hard to feel real love and search

For real love but still my heart
Fears rejection from not being
Any woman's selection and for
So many years I as a man would

Just break down and just cry
Like the emotional rainbow
And at times my very soul felt
Like it would just die like the

Emotional rainbow butterfly because
Like jodeci I to as a man will cry for
You and only you black women because
I just want to be a man after your own

Heart and I pray that from me you will
Never part because being in love with you
Is something that I do exceptional well
Because my love for you is all encompassing

And to my love there is
No end couldn't you tell?
And it's at this point in my
Life that I can no love

Stay in the realities of all
My pain and hurt and not
Go out into this world to
Show the world all of my

Love because I can no
Longer stand on the side
Lines and be shy because
Me and all of my

Emotions must rise like
The emotional rainbow
Butterfly in life's big blue
Sky

Wasted Off Of Your Love

Look black women everything that I have and
Everything that I ever could be as a man
I give to you because you are my heaven on
Earth and no other woman could ever

Replace you because one of a kind
And me even a day without your loving
And affection would cause my very soul
To cry and if you ever walked out of my

Life I would just die because you are a
More than this whole world woman to me
And no other woman could take your place
Nor even begin to match your beauty and grace

Because your love is greater than any other women
Love and your love for me is more than I could ever
Want and I just want to be alone in your love because
You where truly sent from above truly gods greatest gift

To a man like me and I need you and you need me and
Every day of my life I thank god for you and I could not
Even imagine what my life would be without you because
Ever since you came into my life you have shown me what

Love truly is and what love truly could be and that is
All I've ever really wanted to have in my life and

I'm truly thank that I can spend
Any amount of time with you
And that I can forever get wasted
Off of your love because you

Are my Beyoncé and I will
Forever be drunk off of your
Love and it will always be more
Than enough for me because

More than this world is what
You mean to me and this is
Something that no amount of
Time could ever change forever

Wasted off of your love and your love
Alone always

My Love for You is Irreplaceable

Look to all the beautiful black women
With beautiful black skin and brown eyes

And if I didn't have you around in
My life id be and feel like I was nothing
Because all of your skin and its many tones
Are just irreplaceable just like all of my love

For you because I as a man have so much
Love for you and I have so much love to
Give you since I'm being honest with you
With each and every bit of emotional

Transparency that as a man can give and my
Love longs to adorn you and shield from
All of life's scorn because the last thing that
A man like me would want to see is you mourn

Because I've played the lovers game and I've lost
But my heart is still on the battle field and in my very
Heart is where you can shed all of your heartache
And break and all of your concerns and all of your

Fears because without
Your love to fill this void
Of mine my heart
Would just turn into stone

Because your loving is all
That I've ever known and
Everything that I've said
About black women I have

Always shown and indeed
My love for you black
women is irreplaceable
Because real females

Like you are all I truly need
And so I let nothing in all
Creation impede on our
Truly and heavenly love

Because what we have
Was made in god's love
Decreed and know this
Heart of mine is finally freed

Amazing

Black women from the bottom of my heart
All I've ever wanted was you because I've
Always wanted to see you in the rays of your
Endless majesty and shine because your so

Amazing to me and your so incredible and
Irreplaceable to me and beyond divine to me
And each and every time I think about you
All I can do is think about you being and becoming

In time my dreams come true and how I can be all the
Man, that you would ever need for me to be because I just
Want for you to be all mines and I want me to be all yours
And all this love that I have for you I want and need for you

To make it last forever and always because I need for one of you
Lovely and special black women to be my one and only women in
    my life
For all time because black women my love for you goes even deeper
    than the
Roots ever could and you black women are everything that could or
    ever will

Make a man like me happy because you are the incomparable and
    more than
Remarkable treasure that I as a man hold close to my heart
Because again you are and will always be more than
Amazing to me and will always be to my future baby this one is
    for you

I Couldn't Say

Black women I as a man couldn't say that
I don't love you because that would just
Be to much for me and my heart to take
And I couldn't say that I didn't want and need

You and all of the love and affection that you
Would ever give because then this vulnerable
Heart of mine would just break because I love
You more than I love for myself and I love the way

That you've always shined and every time I think
About you I think you being all that I've been to find
And I could never leave all of what you as a woman
Bring to the table behind because you've been everything

That I've ever conveyed because you have always displayed
All of the traits and characteristics that I want and need for a
Woman to have and all of these feelings and emotions that you
Make me feel keeps me in cloud nine and gives me those feelings

Of having these butterflies that I couldn't even begin to explain
Because its my love for you that my heart mind and soul couldn't
Even begin to contain and I couldn't say that you don't mean every
Thing to me because nothing in this world that I could love more
   than I love you

We Should Be Close

And we should be together with our hearts being as one
And have a relationship so pure and loving with true shine
Because black women you are my heart my love and my sun

In your arms black women is where I as a man want to run
To because you are the definition of the heavens clay and wonders
    so lovely and so fine
And we should be together with our hearts being as one

And black women you are second to no one for none
Compare to you because I admire you as woman and your very
    beauty and design
Because black women you are my heart, my love and my sun

And when I'm around you black women I feel like I'm the only man
    in the world that has won
This prize and this treasure because I am yours and you black women
    are all mine
And we should be together with our hearts being as one

And the chapters of my life is where my love for you black women
    has truly begun
And with love like this that I have for you black women how could
    it ever decline
Because black women you are my heart my love and my sun

And in the light and unending rays of you love is where I as a man
    have had the most fun
Because I know that you black women are real women that have a
    backbone and spine
And we should be together with our hearts being as one
Because black women you are my heart my love and my sun

To And Fine

And black women I was made to love you and to see you always shine
And you are such a special part of all that is me
Because in my eyes you my love are to and fine

And there's not a woman on this earth that could have been made
any more divine
Because you allowed someone like myself to finally take fight and
be free
And black women I was made to love you and to see you always shine

Because I am truly yours and you are truly mine
And for your loyalty love and honor alone I will gladly stand on
bended knee
Because in my eyes you my love are to and fine

And because you where crafted in the heavens clay ever known you
were made beautiful in design
And in my life, you were planted like a tree
And black women I was made to love you and to see you always shine

And the definition of what a proverbs 31 woman is what you will
always define
And be defined as because you are my open door and I am your man
and I've got the master key
Because in my eyes my you my love are to and fine

And no greater worth and being could be given to another other
woman combine
Because only someone like you can sail within the heart of my
loving sea
And black women I was made to love you and to see you always shine
Because in my eyes you my love are to and fine

81

Mesmerized

Black woman you leave me so mesmerized beyond what my words
   could ever say
Because your personality grace beauty and charm is what I will
   forever love on any given day
And I get so caught in my feelings when it comes to you
And without you in my life what would I as a man do

When you fill my stomach with those lovers' butterflies
And everlasting paradise filled highs
Because everyday when I'm with you it feels like heavens glory
And with you and you alone is with whom I want to have a forever
   story

With because you are all the woman that I could in this lifetime
And I can only say this in so many words before the end of this very
   rhyme
Because again babe you leave me so mesmerized
And that is why my heart mind body and soul feel so energized

See this once lonely heart that I once had is what you have allowed
   to once again shine
And therefore, you will always be my baby and my everything
   because your so fine
And everything that I must give will come sincerely from the bottom
   of my heart
Because there will never be a day where I would ever want to see
   you part

Because when I was in my feelings drowning in emotional darkness
   of night
You came into this life of mine and became my everlasting and unfading
   light

Because being alone is what hurts the most along with not having
    someone who I can share
All this love and affection with until I met you and know I can declare

What true love is and means again because true love does not lie
And that is why I had had to open my heart to it all again and give
    it another try

Poetic Ballads

True emotions is what I as a man have always
Faced when writing these beautiful and elegant
Poetic ballads that I seem to have embraced because
I've been longing to love and to hold and to know black women
Who I could give my heart mind and soul to as these very?
Tears of mine begin to flow because all I've ever wanted and
Needed was the love that I could never seem to find now is it
Me or is it that love is blind when it comes to females loving on
Someone like me and maybe it's a worldwide thing when all I
Want is for your love to shine upon me so I can hold it close
And love it wild as raindrops fall from the heavens sky as these poetic
Ballads do from my heart to yours because I want you to know that I
Want you to be all mine for all time bright like days and mysterious
Like the dark nights and it is on beautiful lovers in whom I as a man
Have set my sights along with my poetic ballads trying so hard to
    reach
Even higher and higher heights

You Could Be

To all the black women in the world
Wide you could my forevermore
And you could be the very heavenly
Majesty that knocks at my door

And you could be my very heart love
And emotions and inner feelings that
All lie within my negro core and you
Could be the paradise at my very shore

And again, you could be the very reason
Why I as a man even have love to even
Talk about or even to truly explore like
A bird that was made to love and made to

Soar and you could the answer to my call
And you could be my saving grace and you
Could be my hope in a hopeless and empty
Place and you could be the reason why my Heart

Starts to race and you could be all the woman
That I as a man need to embrace because I don't
Want to be the kind of man who puts his heart out
There only to end up in the void of an empty space

And you could be the only face
That I as a man would only want
To see and you could be my
Personal selection because we

Could possibly have a connection
Because you be and really you already
Are perfection and again to all the
Black women worldwide I hope that

You can see all of this in due time
Within this poem and true
Reflection and personal
Introspection and this to me

Is all you beautiful black women
could be or should be oh well
Maybe I just know what I want
and it might just be all of you

The Love Letters Part one

Black women did you get the love letters that I enclosed with my kiss
Oh, and did you get all of them in the nick of time
And did they ever cause you to ever wonder and reminisce

Because all I want you to have is my love my heart and unending
eternal bliss
Because you black women will always be my treasured and certified
dime
Black women did you get the love letters that I enclosed with my kiss

Because what greater time in my life could all of this
Love affection and wonder could ever even reach its prime
And did they ever cause you to ever wonder and reminisce

Because everyday in my eyes is a new and bright genesis
Because of you black women being in it along with the worth and
glory of this very rhyme
Black women did you get the love letters that I enclosed with my kiss

And as long as you black women remain in my life things will never
go amiss
Nor grow sour and fade away in taste like a lemon or even a lime
And did they ever cause you to ever wonder and reminisce

And I could never have the heart to say goodbye as if my name was
Chris
Because I love you black woman and there are still some mountains
that we together must climb
Black women did you get the love letters that I enclosed with my kiss
And did they ever cause you to ever wonder and reminisce

The Love Letters Part Two

And black women all I'm really saying is that this is the love letters
    part two
Because I as a man I'm trying so hard to reach and claim your loving
    warmth and grace
And all I can think of is all the love and affection that I as a man
    want to give to you

And so, you should expect a man like me to always come correct
    when I come through
Why because what good is love if there's no embrace
And black women all I'm really saying is that this is the love letters
    part two

Because black women I just want to be the man that can give you
    the heavens dew
And I want you to do things your way and for you to have your space
And all I think of is all the love and affection that I as a man want
    to give to you

Because black women all the love that I have for you is brighter than
    a day brand new
And you are that special part of me that no other woman could ever
    replace
And black women all I'm really saying is that is the love letters
    part two

And black women there's nothing greater than a proverbs 31 woman
in my view
Because that's the type of woman that you are and have always been
and must chase
And all I think of is all the love and affection that I as a man want
to give to you

And with all that being said my love for you as black women has
truly grew
Because my heart longs to forever run this lover's race
And black women all I'm really saying is that is the love letters
part two
And all I think of is all the love and affection that I as a man want
to give to you

The Love Letters Part Three

Black women can I once again enter the very rooms of your heart for
the love letters part three
Because when you're in that darkest places in your life I as a man
want to be your light
And if you have ever had love for a man like me please just say that
you agree

Because Black women it is in your life that I want to be planted in
like a tree
Along with loving on you and as a man all I want to do is respect you
and treat you right
Black women can I once again enter the very rooms of your heart for
the love letters part three

And if I truly desire to have your heart and trust then this is all you
will ever see
And black women you are the greatest thing that I as a man could
ever see in view of my sight
And if you have ever had love for a man like me please just say that
you agree

Because black woman want you and your soul to be forever free
From any heart ache break and pain and from anyone or anything
that such things to ever ignite
Black women can I once again enter the very rooms of your heart for
the love letters part three

And my love and praise for your glory and majesty is what I will forever decree

And declare because I want to be the kind of man that can bring you comfort in the night

And if you have ever had love for a man like me please just say that you agree

Because you black woman bring so much love into my life and fill my heart with so much glee

And I promise you that it is you and your emotions that I as a man will never smite

Black women can I once again enter the very rooms of your heart for the love letters part three

And if you have ever had love for a man like me please just say that you agree

The Love Letters Part Four

And black women this for you and all those ladies who just want
some more
And I pray that with this poem that I as a man can bring some light
into your dark skies
Because these ladies are my precious love letters and this is the love
letters part four

And black women I just hope that take away all the hurt and pain that
you've carried in your core
Because I truly treasure you and the beauty of worth and elegant rise
And black women this is for you and all those ladies who just want
some more

Of a true man like myself that will always worship the ground you
walk on and adore
You forever and wipe away the very tears that have ever fallen from
your beautiful brown eyes
Because these ladies are my precious love letters and this is the love
letters part four

Because I Elijah Jones want to be the man who alone stands at the
very heart of your shore
So that I as a man can help you reach your endless highs
And black women this is for you and all those ladies who just want
some more

Because I want to be a man after your heart and be worthy enough
to open the door
To your heart because I promise you, I will not ever break your heart
nor feed you lies
Because these ladies are my precious love letters and this is the love
letters part four

And I hope and pray that I as a man have made you as black women feel as if your heart could soar

Because black women your so incredible to me truly a dream come true just like a prize

And black women this is for you and all those ladies who just want some more

Because these ladies are my precious love letters and this is the love letters part four

The Better Man

Black women I just want your heart
Like your last man or should I say
Your last man could never want your
Heart and black women I need your heart

Like your last and past me could ever
Need your heart because I don't want
There to be a single doubt nor thought
In your mind that questions whether or not

I want and need your love because black
Women I crave your love and I long for your very
Touch and black women you just don't know
How much I need every part bit and piece of

You around me because I need you to understand
That this can't be a would have should have or even
A could have thing especially when I'm so open and
Ready to make you black women my everything and

Truly be the type of man that your last man just
Could and would never be for you and your loving
And open heart because your love and your everything
Is all encompassing and truly everlasting because I feel as

Though I could truly be
Better than all of the past
Me in your life and all
They could ever be and

And even this is
Something that the blind
See just I want and need
You black women because I

Honestly believe that
I'm the one who can
Say for a fact that I am
The better man

More Than My Everything

Look without black women like you
In my life I as a man would be
Left feeling so incomplete and without
A woman like you how could I as a man

Truly concrete when I need all of you in
My life and in these confessions of my feelings
As a man pouring out anything and everything out
To you because I more than care for you and therefore

I as a man want to spend my whole life with you
Because you truly are more than my everything and I
Will forever need you to shine down your light upon me
So that my blind eyes can see what a real woman looks like

Because it will always be you who will forever shine so bright and
     to the
Darkest of places in my heart mind and soul you being
The proverbs 3 I woman can be the light that I as a man
Need because again you are more than my everything and to

A woman like you is who I as a man give my everything
To and surrender unto you that special part of who I am
Because when I am with you, I no longer feel as though I have
To guard this lonely heart of mine

More Beautiful Than Heaven Itself

Oh black women days without you being in this life
Of mine are just days that I can't afford because
Baby you are my greatest treasure and reward
That I could ever want and need to have as mine

And each part of the proverbs 31 woman
That I know is within you is all that I ever seem to
Move toward and your endless grace and majesty
Is what I as a real man will never leave ignored because

Baby to me you mean more than life itself to
Me and you are more beautiful than the heavens themselves
And you are more than worthy to be worshipped and adored
And every time I'm around you I stand in awe of you because

You leave me so mesmerized that my words couldn't even begin to
Describe everything that I'm feeling or thinking about when
It comes to you and when I'm come down from cloud nines
Skies and having butterfly in my stomach feeling I begin to

Think about the possibilities of love not yet explored
And baby you have more than restored my lost faith in
Love and what I as a man thought it once was because being
And feeling like I'm in love truly means everything to me

And this is why to me you
Will always be more beautiful
Than heaven itself and in my
Mind body and soul is where

My love for you and affection
For you will forever remain
Stored because again baby you
Truly are more beautiful than

Heaven itself and you will
Always be

Beauty

Black women your beauty and your grace is
So much more than any man could even
Imagine or even want and baby this is what
Your beauty and your beauty alone has ever

Defined and baby you were truly made and
Are worth more than any piece of silver and gold
Because to me you are the greatest thing that could
God himself could have ever designed and you will

Always have my heart and will always be the
Greatest thing to have ever entered into and I thank
God for even creating you and you're all that I want as
A man and I thank god for all that he has ever made you

To be and every part of me longs and cries for you and
Every part of me I give to you from every beat of my heart
To the depths of my being and soul as a man and who and what
I am as a man belongs to you and you alone and your beauty is what

Could never be ignored because I as a man couldn't afford to
Not have you as my greatest reward that I will forever treasure and
Hold on to for all time because you have the true beauty that lies on
The inside and out because your beauty in my eyes will always have a

Rise because your beauty never
Cries because your beauty is
And will always me everything
To me from the bottom of my heart

Can Your Heart Still be Mine?

Black women without you and all
Your love my heart could
Never even begin to shine
And if anything, happen between

Us could your heart still be mine
And I know that we all say and
Do things in the heat of the moment
But that still was never a reason to

Ever cross your very line and bae
Just know that I love you and without
You all I am is just a man without a
Spine and know I'm forever in search of

And relentlessly looking for hope that I
Can't seem to find ever since you left me
And my heart behind and without you
I feel as though my heart has been played

And I feel so damn betrayed by you
And by all of life's shade to and I feel so
Much heartache that my very soul feels
As though it might break and uncontrollably

It starts to shake and
Slowly fade away and if
Poem could not convey
This to you what more

Can I as a man even say
Or do but cry out until
The end of time can your
Very heart still be mine

Forever In Your Eyes

Oh, black women you truly are the answer to all
Of my cries and everything that I as a man
Could ever want and need is all in between those
Thighs and so I will forever value it and you as I

Begin to fantasize about it and how I as a man
Could possible see forever in your eyes because
Your so incredible to me and now my once blind
Eyes can now truly see endless highs that only you

Alone can bring and this a feeling and a love that
I as a man will never compromise because once I
Was a foolish man and how I am so wise because?
Once I was a foolish man and now, I am so much

Wiser because it had taken many years but know
The time has come for you and me baby to be as one
As sure as the sun and the moon and the stars remain
So bright you baby will always and forever be my one

And only personal light and in saying all of this
I will continue to emphasize that I as a man will
Now and forever see
The beauty in your eyes

You Make Me Feel Like

Black women you make me feel like more
Than a man who could more than open
His heart mind and soul to you and you
Make me feel the feeling of what it truly

Means to be in love because I've truly never
Felt a love and a trust like this and I never
Felt that I could feel something for anyone
Until the very day that I as a man met you

And having all these feelings or even being
With someone else other than you are something
That I as a man just could not even begin to imagine
Because your love for me is to kind and its true and it

Makes me as a man want everything about you even more
Because you feel like I can be loved and cared for and that
I as a man no longer must feel lonely have to feel because
I know that I feel something for you, and I know that you feel

Something for me and you make me feel like you
Could be more than I could ever talk about or even
Dream about is what you make a man like me
Feel like and that is something that will never change

So Much Love In My Heart

In all of creation I could never even begin
To find nor will I ever find more lovely and
More amazing than black women because there's
No other females like you and for you there is so

Much love in my heart for you and only you
And the thought of it all is just taking over me
My mind and my inner thoughts and feelings that
I as a man have for you and could only share with you

Alone and every time I think about heaven and its
Sunshine and every bit of sunshine that could come
From it all because you are the definition of what paradise
Is and that is the heaven that I see within you because again I have

So much love in my heart for you black women each and everyday
Of my life feel so damn brand new and what other female in all
Creation could I as a man have love for that remains so true when
I already have so much love in my heart for you black women like you

And since I have so much love in my heart for you
Could you give me the same type of love back to me?
And have so much love in your heart for a man like me
Forever and ever cause as a man I just need to know

A Poem To Heather Headley

Heather Headley thank you for being the kind of
Woman who knows how to show love to a black man
And heather Headley that you being the kind of woman
That a real man would want and treasure and Heather Headley

Thank you for your songs and words of hope when I thought
That there was none left and thank you for being the melanin
Queen that god has made you to be and though my eyes were once
Blind now they can see that beautiful black women like you are the

Only kind of women for me and I am truly thankful you and every
Breathe that you take and I am thankful for every move that you make
And now I realize that I only want black women like you and nobody
Else and thank you for all the love and warmth that your music and
     words

Provide and thank you for helping walk less in pride
And your song he is helped me understand who that black man
Within me is and your song helped me to understand who you
Are and how your love for black men runs so deep and now I
     understand

Why my heart will always be that one thing that black
Woman like you will always keep and to understand who he is
Is to understand who you are as beautiful black women and
Queens 25 years and now I see how you have always been there
     for me

My Heart Cries For You

Look as sure as the heavens rain down
Their majestic dew my heart alone cries for
Black women and black women alone know and
Always because black women you are the glue

That holds a man like myself together because you've
Been and every little thing that I as a man wanted and
Needed you to be for me and you have always been so loving
And so kind and women like you are so hard to find and black women

Like you have always been so true, and this is why my heart
Cries for you and everything that I am and am willing to give
I give to you my heart you can have it my emotions my feelings
My being love you black women you can have it all because you

Are my forever lady and the very light within my view because?
You cared for me when I didn't even care for myself or about myself
And you loved on me when I didn't even love myself and that is why
My very heart cries for you and only back are your sin scars and

Transgressions that I will forever bare because you carne into this
Lonely heart of mine with so much love to give and share and because
Of that my heart from the very depths of my being as a man
Cries for you because black women my heart forever cries for you

So Open And So Ready

Black women I just want you and I need
You to not just my anything but my
Everything because my mind soul
Emotions and being are so open and so

Ready to be loved on by you and only
You because what other female can love
Me in the same way that you do and
Black women I need you and only you

Because I can't need other females like I
Need you because my heart mind soul and
Being is so open and so ready for you and you
Alone and these are just my personal confessions

Of who I give my everything to and who I could
Never give all my love and everything to if the girl isn't
Black women like you who I as a man show all my expressions
Of love to even in the midst of my racial transgressions I will

Forever declare this and no matter where my mind
Is when writing in these poetic sessions I will forever
Share this because again black women my heart mind and soul and
Being longs and needs to be loved on by you and only you

I Adore you

Know I can say that as a black man
That I am a lover of black women worldwide
That I will always and forever adorn you and
Treat you black women like the beautiful jewel that

You are and have always been so that I as a man
Never have to play the Jesters position as the fool
Because black women I really and truly adore you and
Love you and how you brighten up my day and in

My personal view I cry out for you because as a man
I let myself be emotional vulnerable when I'm around you because
My heart cries for you and with you black women I want
To go places that no other female that I've been with has

Ever been before and I want it to be just us together as we
Go to open that very door with our emotions and hearts
As one because on the other side black women lies the realities
Of paradise everlasting and when I'm with you alone I can finally

Share all that I have hidden on the inside because you took
The time to read my life's book and for that I will forever adore
You and you are right where I want to be because at the core of who
I am you are all I can see and all that I will forever want to see
    and until

Drive and Ambition

Black women I want to love
You with all my ambition and
All my drive because when I'm
With you I feel so free and so

Alive because your love is sweeter
That bees in a bee hive and you alone are
My personal honey and I want you to
Know that my love for you is beyond

Concrete along with my lover's heart that nothing could in this
World could ever deplete, and I pray that
Each and every day god will
Allow me to knock you off your feet

With all my drive and ambition that will
Never break nor bend because I promise to
Love you and I care for you until the very end
Know forevermore because when I was down it

Was you alone who brought light into this lonely
Heart of mine so that my heart would continue
Would shine and without any debate it will
Always beyond and your very heart and I as a man

Will forever want you to be
The fuels and the ignition to
All my drive and ambition
Because it's all yours black women

I'm a Slave To Your Sweet Love

Black women as a man I'm a slave to
Your sweet love because at the table of
Your love and emotions alone is where I
As a man and as a man who longs to be a man

After your heart will always and forever be
Seated and black women without your love I
Could not go on because my heart would be
Much to make it on its own because without

You black women all I am is just a man in his
Feelings that are forever deep in thoughts drowning
Of you and all that we could be but what we are not all
Yet are and that is what at times makes me so heated

And so, I run to find someone or something that
Can find this void of mine but yet at the end of the
Day I just end up running back to you because I just
Want to be loved and I don't want to end up hurt again

And with no other female could I find the joys of being
In love again to have and to hold and to feel and to be real
With and know other female could have treated a man like
Me with real love and respect like you black women do and for

Reasons I will always be a slave
To your sweet love and your
Sweet love alone because even
My heart said don't go don't go

Because Elijah you might only
End up in that place that your
Once called woe and the feeling
Of defeated hurts to much

And being so emotional
Vulnerable hurts even more
With my pride especially
When there are no more tears

left to be cried and nothing
Could ever change this
Forsaken tide and I say all
To say that I hope you

Can be my everything
Because I just want to a
Slave to your sweet
Love forevermore

I Feel Worthless Without You

Black women without someone
Like you how could I as a man
Even begin to have worth or
Value and black women without

Someone like you what in this world
Would I as a man even really pursue
Or even have to pursue because without
Your loving touch I as a man would feel

So worthless because I need someone
Who will care for me and I need someone
Who will be there for me because I couldn't
Live my life without you because your all

I need and more and it took me many years
To figure this all out but I want to make you
The love of my life and the very light of my
World and to share in all the love and joy with

Females like you and only you and I've realized
That I cannot go on unless I have you because what
Is a man without a female like you because if you
Weren't in my life my life would truly feel so lonely

And worthless without you
Because you are the only one
For a man like me and I couldn't
My life without you

Share My World

I'm my introspective views I am
Confessing to you that the feeling of being
In love is truly a blessing because love can
Make you feel as though it was only the season

Of spring especially when you that you've found
A good thing because and that is my
Beautiful Beatrice the woman that I as a man
Would give my very life to because I truly love

Her and there's nothing in this world that I
Wouldn't do for a woman like her because when
I'm truly with her I feel no more heart ache and
When I'm with her my heart doesn't feel like it's about

To break and on my back are her sins that I will
Forever bare because my heart belongs to her
And all that I could ever declare is this world
And this life that I will forever share because I

Am all hers and she is all mine and with her and
Her alone is who I share my world with and
That is you black women and you black women
Alone

An Ode to Black Women

From the very bottom of my being
As a man and as a human being I love
You black women and if I didn't have black
Women in my heart and deep within the depths

Of my very mind and at the core of my human
Soul what other race of female could make a man
Like me feel so complete and this is why I as a man
Will always love you and this is why I as a man will

Always need you because black women you love is and
Will always be sweet to me because I want to be down with
All you beautiful black women around me and this is some
Thing that will never change because black women are the

Type of girls that I as a man will pour my very heart out to
Because black women, my love for you is like an everlasting
Fire and you, black women will be all that a man like me will
Desire because my love for you is bold and my love for black

Women is like having riches untold and my love for you is
All that I as a man feel and I'm not playing when I say this be my feelings
For you are all too real and this is how I as a man truly feel about you
And this very poem is an ode to beautiful black women like you

The Realities Of Your Clay

Black women to you and you
Alone are the women in whom
I as a man call my everything
Because you're always in my heart

And on my mind and on my mind is
Where you always seem to stay and no
Matter what happens you will always
Have a say in my life because you're more than

Wonderful and amazing and your very
Being is just indescribable to me and
I will forever love your kingdom crafted
Skin tone and your beauty that a man like

Me could only hope to grace within the many realms
Of your throne because black women you are the
Greatest thing that god has or ever will make
And has ever designed along with your chocolate skin

And your personality charm
Beauty and being and clay that I as a black man
Love so damn much and the very bones that carry
It all and this is what the realities of your very clay

That I as a man will always and
Forever chase because the realities
Of your clay isn't just something
That I as a man could ever replace

Because the realities of your clay
Mean everything to me and it's all I
Want and will forever need and will
Always embrace

Because what other female in all
Creation could make my heart
And love feel so special
And so grounded in true love

Let Me Be The Clay

To each and every black women worldwide
I just have one question to ask today and that
Is can you let me be the clay on your potter's
Wheel in which you love, and can you let me

Be all that you will ever need, and can I be
Your very light when you f-eel like yours just
Wont shine and can I hold you and can I need
You and be forever wrapped up in your loving

Arms that can shield me from all of life's hurt
And all its pain because I need you and I want
You because what is my life without you in
When I as a man have been looking and searching

To find black women like you who can hold me and
Embrace me because black women you have my very
Heart in your hands and so again what I'm saying is
Can you let me as a man be all the clay that you will?

Ever want and need because I can be that me
My heart can be that for you and my body can be
That you and my being can be that for you and you
Only because this poem like many others is for your eyes only

If you black women will let
A man like me be all the
Clay that you mold on your
Potter's wheel forever yours

The Year Of The Real Man

Black women I know that
You're not looking for a boy
Because you need a real man
With a true plan with real goals

And you need the type of man
Who will never in this lifetime
Cast you nor your emotions feelings
And inner pain and heartache aside

Because a real man would care about
You more than his own pride and you
Need a man who won't cheat on you
With all these other females out here
someone

In these streets because if he really loves
You then he will do all that he can just for you
Because black women your love was and could
Never be misplaced and I see that your love was

True and if a man can't understand that then he never
Really loved you but your man could never see that because
He was so busy looking at other females in his view
And he failed to realize that none of those females

Could ever be you
Nor do all of the
Little things that only
You can do

Because your man is
A player still acting like
A boy playing in the sand
But what you really

Needed was a man who
Wouldn't play around
With you or your heart
And you needed

Who would take the lead
And at the same time
Lend you a hand and you
Realized that play time is

Over and know its time
For the year of the
real man to be real and
open enough to stand up

The Final Love Poem

Black women you know that
You and only you in all your
Everlasting glory but know the
Time has come for me to end that

Story with this is the final.
Love poem because all good things
Must come to an end but in my heart
And soul is where you black woman will

Forever remain and the thought of this
Being the very last poem that I as a man
Ever write to you or about you truly hurts
Because all my feelings and emotions for

You are so complicated, and it is your love
That for so long I've only advocated for and
I've been so captivated by your being and love
So strong and I'm so sad that this is the end because

You black women where my hope my escape from
Anything and everything because my life you
Were beloved and long awaited and this is something
That will never be debated and even though I must let

You go, and you will forever be
Celebrated and so this poem
Ends the chapter
Of black women

With the final
Love poem just know that I
Love you and that I as a man
Care you and your heart black women

I Want Your Heart Pt. 2

Black women I just want your
Heart like know other man could
Ever want your heart and black women
I need your heart know other man

Could ever need you heart because I as
A man need to find your love even if
it costs me my very life because it's that
Feeling of wanting and needing and you

That I as a man could never part from
Because again I want your heart and I just
Want to drown in the pools of your
Everlasting love and I'll go to hell and back

For you because for the sake of your love
I will be your Dante and you can be my Beatrice
Because without you my soul is and means nothing
And the damned can't have you because as a man and

As your man want all of you because I'll always
Want and need your heart until all of time ends
I'll still want and need you and your heart because
I couldn't imagine even a day with you in my life

God Reveal My Heart to Her

God I just want special black women
To know that I love her and that
And as her man I want to show her
That I really care because this is the

Year of the gentleman and my love
For her is what I must have, and give and it is
Also, something I must declare because
I need her, and I appreciate her because

She completes me truly and she holds
My heart in her hands and this is something
That I need to for her to understand so god
Can you please just reveal my heart to her because

She my everything and I need her to be my
Everything and she is my ride or die and my very
Best friend and lover and even the blind can see
That she will always ride with me and for me

But lately we've been going through somethings and
Things between us have shifted and have changed
And it makes me feel so damn bad on the inside that
It hurts my heart and my very pride even though I'm going

Through all this god
Please reveal my true
Heart to her because I
Must let her know that

Love her so because I as a man
Could never and would
Never let her and her love
Just go

Not Even The Heavens Stars And Gates

Truly not even the heaven nor
The stars and its many gates truly
Appreciates the true love found in
Your very grace and until you die

I will forever embrace all of your
Worth and honor with no debates
Because the day in which I stop
Loving you black women that is the

Day when I will see everlasting disgrace
Along with what I thought and had believed
Was your unfading love gone without a trace?
And again, not even the stars and its many gates

Could ever truly allow you to shine nor
Celebrates each and every little thing that
You and your being creates and then demonstrates
A truly powerful change in my life because its type

Of change that this world even seen and for
You and you alone I will forever fiend for your
Heart being mind and soul because not even the heavens
Stars and gates have anything on you black woman

One Time For Your Heart

Black women its one time for your heart
That I could never forsake and one time for
Your heart that I could never break and if it is
Not my love for you in which I know share

Then I'd rather live my life in utter agony and
Despair and its one time for your heart that
Should never be played and its one time for
Your heart that should never be betrayed because

Your beauty grace worth an honor gives me
A really good feeling and fills me with great Joy
And further fuels my endless drive and romantic
Prose and like rain and sun t a beautiful rose your

Being alone takes away all my woes and its one
Time for your heart that keeps my mind and soul
At bay like lakes and quiet streams because you end
What feels like disarray in my life and its one time for

Your heart that has been these poems very theme and its
One time for your heart that know is more than just
A dream because these feelings and the emotions that I
Display are all for you and that feeling is all too real for me

Printed in the United States
By Bookmasters